Breath Found Along the Way

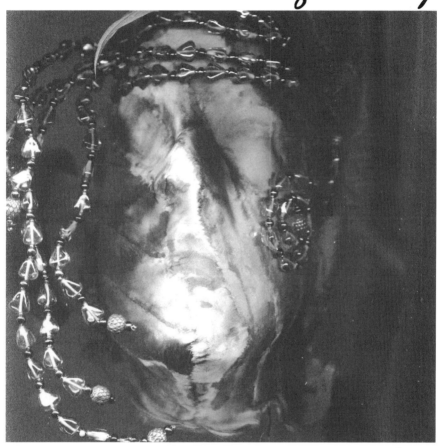

Anne Schneider

To Janet –
best wishes along
The Way
Anne Schneider
7-4-03

Plain View Press
P. O. 33311
Austin, TX 78764

plainviewpress.com
sbright1@austin.rr.com
1-800-878-3605

Front cover and title page: "Phantom," plaster gauze, screened-print silk, Egyptian glass beads, brass beads, feathers.

Back cover: Memorial Service, *Virgen de Guadalupe* mask. Photo by Don Murray

Acknowledgements

Many thanks to the editors of the following publications where these poems first appeared:

"Diving," **Armadillo**, The Maverick Press; "Swiss Army Knife," **Mind the Gap**, New York/London, Issue Four 2000; "Mama's House," **Summer Shade**, Quill Books; "Christmas Carol," **Texas Poetry Calendar 2000,** Flying Cow Productions; "Forgotten Bouquet," **Texas Poetry Calendar 2002,** Flying Cow Productions; "Alphabet Soup," **Texas Writer September 2001**, Writers' League of Texas; "White Fire," **White Tail**, The Maverick Press; "Mother's Day" and "Nesting Borders," **Womankind,** Anderie Poetry Press.

Introduction

Almost five years ago my *sifu*, a *Tai Chi* master, died suddenly. *Sifu* Steven Kronnick's death left his many students with a fervent desire to know, to call by name that which had become so essential in their lives. A beloved student asked, "What is *Tai Chi?*"

Sifu Dr. Clay L. Cox looked up from sorting a box of his friend and former student's personal belongings. He answered with kind eyes and a smile, "To me *Tai Chi* is the Breath I found along the Way." His brief, full-of-wisdom answer still inspires me today. I could choose no better title for this book, as my practice of *Tai Chi* and the whole of my life experiences are truly "breath found along the way."

My poetry and my masks are the sweet exhalation of that breath.

I was first introduced to mask making four years ago at a small retreat not far from my home in the Texas Hill Country. Four women spent Halloween weekend in a private home, supporting each other's journey of self-discovery. That first night we cast each other's faces, completely entrusting ourselves to the hands of friends. Soft music, incense, and gentle massage soothed our busy minds and tired bodies. As the plaster gauze layers were smoothed over our faces, sensory perceptions heightened beneath masks from which we could not see or speak. Assisted by caring loved ones in removing our cast mask, holding it at last in our own hands, was akin to receiving a newborn in our arms for the first time. With awe and wonder, each cradled her own face cast mask.

We spent the rest of the weekend designing and decorating our masks, each creating our own myths along the way. We had brought small treasures to share – old jewelry, shells, beads, feathers, fur. We pooled our resources, fanning the collection across the floor. Hiking later among the rocks and cedar, we gathered gifts Nature offered us as well. We trimmed the tails of horses, collected weeds, seeds, and porcupine quills. As the weekend progressed, we reflected on the evolution of our masks. Their possibilities were limitless. So, too, we understood, were our own possibilities.

That weekend began my quest for an expanded mask experience. The following spring I attended artist Ann Lyneah Curtis' technical face casting workshop. I spent six months researching the history of masks and creating a mask workshop outline and graphic handouts for students.

These past three years I have had the pleasure of conducting workshops across Texas for continuing education classes, camps, family reunions, small parties, conventions, and businesses. I encourage workshop participants to discover their Muse, to focus on self-visions found along the creative way. The delight of participants in their finished masks is a joy I savor at each and every workshop. Words like "I can't" or "I'm not artistic" dissolve when encountered by the inevitable beauty of face cast masks. What greater canvas than the human face could there be for art? What better voice than poetry?

Anne Schneider
October 2002

Memorial Service, "*Virgen de Guadalupe*" mask. Photo by Don Murray

Illustrations

Contents

Special Thanks

Thanks to my husband Harry who always believed I could fly. Thanks to my daughters Rachel Krenek and Lisa Murphy who echo Harry's encouragement to follow my dreams. Thanks to my father Timothy J. Cronin who quoted classical poetry to me when I was a child. Thanks especially to my mother Louise and the rest of my family who may not always understand me (or my poetry), but love me anyway. Thanks to the many special friends who also have been my teachers, mentors, and students along the Way – particularly Sally Alter, Phyllis Garey, Jean Murray, Jim Shelton, and Kevin Van Renterghem. Thanks to the organizations and their talented members who have guided my poetry writing these past seven years: San Antonio's Gemini Ink, the Kerrville Writers Association, Austin's Texas Writers League, and the 2002 Ghost Ranch October Writing Festival. Thanks, finally, to my editor Susan Bright – certainly for her technical support, but especially for her enthusiastic vision for art in the world.

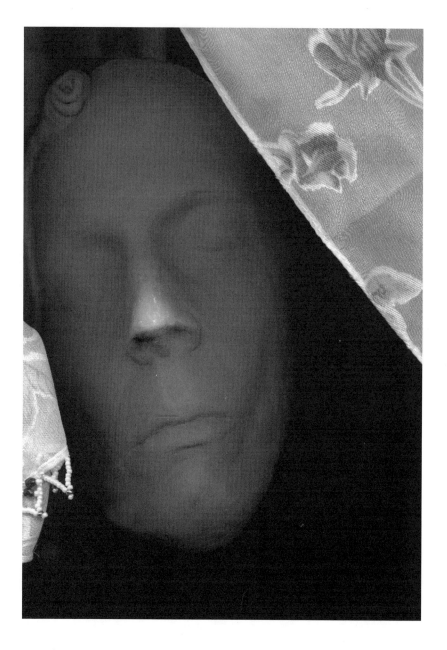

"*Virgen de Guadalupe,*" fired clay (from plaster gauze cast), Reikied beaded scarf by Carol Krause.

Fountain Fantasy

She tosses three coins
to ensure her return
to people and place,
far from her own.

Young dreams
prompt rites,
not understood,
never forgotten.

Diving

thanks to Larry

Tempt me with your offer.
I want to know
places you promise.
Part of me resists,
like a child rejects
the darkness of a closet.

You will teach and I will learn.
I will marvel at the world
you know so well.
I will trust,
then let go of everything
that feels safe.

Hand in hand
we descend together.
We go slowly into the sunless depths,
adjust, foot by foot,
the cool beauty
sealing us in silence.

The soft ballet of a sea fan's sway
soaks me in rhythms
of unheard currents.
Like an impatient child
pleading to be followed,
that dance gently tugs us.

At first all goes well.
I feel I've passed a test,
like the first kiss of adolescence.
But you fail to notice my hand
removed from yours,
my mask beginning to leak.

Quietly,
your world seeps into mine,
across the boundary
I've so carefully set for myself.
Betraying barriers, the cold water
numbs my sense of control.

I struggle to maintain what is mine.
The more you replace me,
the less I can breathe.
If I stay at your side,
unable to ask for the air I need,
I know I will drown.

I jerk the mask from my face,
fight to regain the surface
where light and wave tips flash.
My breath is suffocated
by a world that eludes,
yet crushes me with its weight.

When you turn to share
the brilliance of an angelfish,
you find terror in my face.
You shake your head wildly, side to side,
point to the air hose floating loose behind me.
But my eyes no longer see you.

You grab my arm to block my ascent.
Like a fly rod snapped back in mid-cast,
I come back to you.
You force your piece into my mouth,
I accept the gift, blink back at you,
a man I never knew.

continued

I no longer think about saving myself.
Shared air sustains us both.
The weight of your hand
balances me in the ceaseless current.
My pulse begins to slow, blood flows
like bubbles heading sun-ward.

We rise to clutch the sunlight,
float like fish feeding on the surface.
You search my eyes
desperate to find what I hold inside,
hoping to swim in pools
that collect your passion.

Your smile forms a mask over me,
a shell with new air, new life.
You offer to return me
to where we began,
off in the distance,
past the tide glistening on the beach.

But I refuse a return
to the familiar sand's solitude,
its tide pools reflecting
how little I've learned.
I will wait for a sign, a turn in the tide,
attempt the dive again.

Cinderella

Fairy, god, and mother,
you steal into my room,
unbidden but not unexpected.
You offer me my dreams.
Am I entitled to such grace?
One royal evening suspended in time,
then gone at the stroke of midnight.

Do I accept,
daring to venture
beyond my own fable?
To dress in silk,
wear jewels at my neck,
perfume in my hair?
One starry night
of music and whispers,
a vanishing promise
in the face of the moon,
the chance to flee
in a golden coach.

Your magic surrounds me
spinning dark dreams;
cocoon to butterfly
I begin my brief flight
to one who would love me.
I can feel your music
coaxing my feet
with long-remembered rhythms.
I see my reflection
in the tops of glass slippers —
caterpillar, or butterfly?

Swiss Army Knife

It hides in the back of my jewelry box
beside the gold band slivered with zirconia,
nested in a tooth fairy's collection of tiny pearls

dearly paid for

bloody red finish, the perfect foil
for its silver-cross shield,
just slightly scratched — that cross

begging for a second chance

at salvation, never too late —
a leftover promise
from Catholic schooling,
a gift
from my husband
(first husband)
so I'd always be prepared

I wasn't

(ever any good at math)
multiplication/division —
rogue cells beyond the doctor's reach

and mine

still bleeding,
I test the blade across my finger.

The Way You Drive

I love the way you take charge
of planning our vacation —
which interstates we'll travel,
mile after mile,
where we'll stop for picnics
on sticky concrete tables.

I dream about scenic detours
we always get lost on,
about feasts we share —
chicken-fried steaks at greasy spoons,
about how high your blood pressure is
when we finally get home.

How many times do I have to tell you
I don't mind cross-country road trips?
Who would feel comfortable flying now?
Our luggage would probably get lost,
and waiting on toll roads
beats waiting on runways.

Besides, I love the way
the car's A/C freezes up,
blows that chalky white mist,
refusing to make our little world
comfortable —
it reminds me of the way
you drive.

Post Mortem

I could've mustered more grief
at the time
if it hadn't been squandered

bit by bit

over the years,

a slow leak
leaving me flat
like a tire worn bald
from uneven wear.

Forgotten Bouquets

Arranged around the tiny table
they wilt, too long with too little.
They sway on long-stemmed stools,
sip wine, drink beer
in glasses, smoke
thin cigarettes.

They sow faded stories, tales
of what they'd do if
they had the time,
the money,
the man.

They plant hugs
stunted by moonlight,
perennial goodbyes, dried
seeds scattering
on sidewalks.

Resurretion

I walk barefoot, sun bleaching soul,
drying damp places that threaten decay.
My journey snakes through wind blown
mountains of timeless sand.

Curandera's shadow seeps from my feet,
black river sustaining the oasis.
Coyote's call echoes the deceiving winds
whistling the desert's bounty.

I rise with yuccas above swelling sands,
learn roots seeking moisture grow deeper,
work High Plains magic with woody fingers,
create altars on moonscaped mesas.

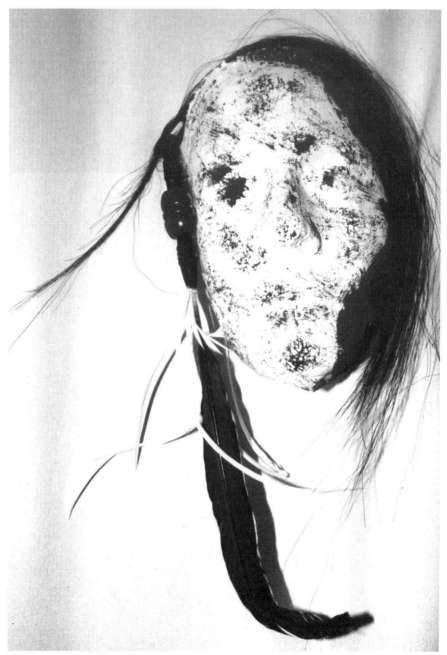

"Guardian," plaster gauze, acrylic paints, horsetail, feathers, wood beads. Donated to Kerrville Independent School District Lifelong Learning Center, November 2001.

Baptism

Child of stone,
harden not your heart.
Surrender your tears,
as rain pours out its grief
when swollen clouds
no longer carry burdens.

Cleanse me of guilt
gnawing at me
with my own teeth.
Child on the moon's dark side,
bear with me,
slide from the crescent
unaware of its own light.

Come with me to wax and wane
with ocean tides, scavenging
beaches like gulls hungry,
hungry now for grace.

Carousel

for Rachel

I watch her approaching thirty
quicker than a horse gone barn-sour.
Same one who thought she'd never be
thirteen, sixteen, twenty-one.
Same one who loved the carousel's
turning, turning, turning
dizzy up-and-down dance,
neon flash of lights,
organ-grinding oompahs.

She's bored beginning,
ending, in the same place,
wants off, wants to explore
carnival corners, remembering
rhythms in a whispering womb.

I watch her grab the ring,
wave good-bye.

Nesting Borders

for Lisa

Selves nest within selves,
each waiting for the full moon,
each emerging with a lust for light,
creating the woman she wants to be.

Crossing boundaries of shifting borders,
a traveler claiming no past,
she jettisons baggage in her wake,
history's subtle persuasions still packed.

Courting strangers in foreign places,
auditions risked for choicest parts,
a star shines, no mirrors, no magic,
in the role she was born to play.

Mother's Day

Breezes blow through trees like traffic in the distance,
the sun seeking places it has never seen.
I lay stripped of all boundaries —
Time. Place. Duty.

Nature nurtures a new child's mother,
basking in the warmth of memories and horizons.
Like a rock, I hold heat against the chill of night —
Quiet. Waiting. Ready.

I imagine the trip home for Mothers' Day,
filled with hugs and tears bridging many miles.
I girl-talk with grown daughters —
Easy. Happy. Knowing.

We get ready for bed, they stare and whisper
Mother, you have no tan lines.
I whisper back *I don't need them anymore* —
Sure. Loved. Loving.

Found at the Altar

Red-tailed hawks parasail my sky
messengers from a world beyond
but within my reach.
From my porch I watch sun
rise on veined roadmaps illuminated
in the ears of jackrabbits.

Hills swell within my rocky womb,
cactus fruit defying
the lack of rain, the refuge
offered in this place
called mine.

I stack stones along my road,
gifts to the grandmothers
walking here before me
straight and balanced,
saluting the sun.

Sunset

Humpbacked hills slice through mist
like whales crossing a blue sea.
Beached sun bleeds a creeping tide,
crimson pools between distant waves.
Clouds float in indigo wash
like squid's ink riding the horizon's reef.

What artist with a sailor's soul
could resist the twilight tempest —
rock perch lure above ocean palette,
wind stirring souls as it chills the skin?
Who dares refuse the sun a goodnight kiss?

The Christmas Coat

for Fred

Frayed edges tempt me
to pull at threads
no longer bound
by warp and woof
of countless weavings
under one roof.

Threads poke heads
of multi-colors
from once-smooth seams,
stubborn refusals
to quit a design
so long ago new,
so fitting.

Christmas, our chance
to claim a place
in the seam of things,
retrace patterns,
embroider relations,
careful not to drop the stitch
no one wants to sew.

We gather for the holiday,
the holy day of toasts
to all those present
no matter match,
remembering those
who in the end,
hung the coat
upon the rack
and walked
into the
cold.

When You Were a Child

Did you ever play God
at night
outside
with a flashlight?

Did you shine
that eye
in the corner
of your own backyard,

illuminating only
that space
before you,

safe

knowing the rest
of the night
does not
exist

beyond the eye
of God?

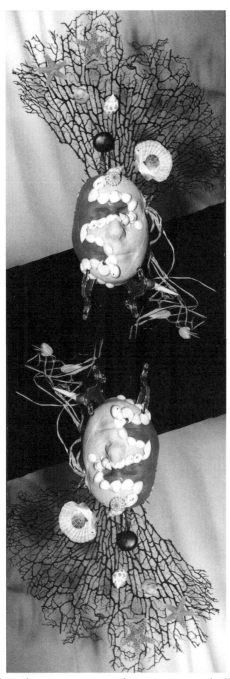

"Sea Nymph," plaster gauze, acrylic paints, sea shells, sea fan, rafia.

Sea Gym

Adolescent mecca
washing over memory

sun, sand, surf,
all in extreme

abandonment
of self to sea,

baptism, by immersion
and true grit.

Graduation

Woman-child beams,
cascade of gold
pours down her black gown.
I stroke the waterfall
thick with memories.

Cap crowns her head,
a square launch pad
tilted toward tomorrows.
We laugh, try to fasten its promise
with bobby pins.

Color cords stream
an honors rainbow,
feats won so far from home.
My chest tightens, swelling
with rain's run-off.

Clutching credentials,
she smiles my smile —
childbirth's tears recycled,
my baby gives birth
to herself.

Time to Talk

The phone rings twice
while I'm outside,
tempting me to untangle
from the snaking
hose around my ankles.
I rely, instead, on my answering
machine, its memory much better
than mine.

Satisfied the sage will recover
from wilting, the salvia
will continue to bloom,
I charm the hose back into a coil,
skate wet porch tiles
to retrieve iced-tea.

Propping bare feet on desktop,
I press the blinking button: both
daughters have called, both
on their way out
the door, into
a busy
day.

Hey, Mom! What's up?
Whatcha doin' this mornin'?
I gotta go . . .

Hi, Mom, it's me. What's on
your agenda today?
I have an appointment . . .

Two daughters, two women,
taking time to check
on me, tell me
where they think they're going.

continued

I watch beads roll transparent
down my glass, thinking,
debating, what to say
when I return
my children's calls.

How I read Rilke as dawn
seeped across the hills?

How I sipped herbal tea,
mind meditating, sending
my love?

How I waited for
hummingbirds to weave
dizzy raids on feeders
I just filled?

How I did slow cat-stretches
to ease the nesting pain
in my back?

How I played with words,
teasing secrets from pages
collecting whispered promises?

No, not on the telephone, I can't
go into how I spent this morning,
or yesterday's, or the one before.

These daughters of mine, already
halfway out their door,
don't have time
to listen.

I call them back
anyway,
leave a message
at the beep.

Hi, Honey, this is Mom.
I haven't been up to much.
Call me when you have time
to talk. I'll just be here
at home.

Mama's House

The house creaks like an old woman's rocker, sighing now
when the wind blows, making peace with a shifting foundation.
Arthritic with termites, my birthright yields in places
where the odd piece of furniture sits upended,
a sinking ship in a sea of rot.

Adrift in rooms empty without her, I search the yard's horizon.
Her dishpan still hangs from the arbor frame, waiting for fruit
from vines gone bare, while license plates nailed
to the washhouse door, tell their stories in rusted letters
of backroads and deadends and journeys long over.

Hydrangeas cluster along the walk where withered blooms
whisper like brittle spinsters, gossiping over the family secrets.
Beneath the black hickory splintered with age, her bathtub lays
grounded, plundered of clawfeet, treasure abandoned
to a shriveled leaf legacy.

Tarpaper raps against the roof, no scarecrow effect
on the homing instincts of pigeons or young women.
Saplings line up under loblolly pines, sailing memories
into tomorrow, of picnics and promises under the trees,
of old women who never leave home.

White Fire

White Shaman,
Speak to me of curly-tailed panthers
and spirits borne on wings of giant blackbirds.
I tremble like a rabbit trapped
in the shrinking shade of sweet acacia,
flame-tipped spears of ocotillo
drawing me to canyon cliffs.
Ceniza's perfume seduces me
into stone-cupped hands of dry arroyos
renewed by rain, blessed by forgotten blossoms.
Yet doubt still pierces,
a shameless gnawing buzzard always with me.
Fear sifts through my veins
like shifting sand in shapeless dreams.

White Shaman,
I hear your Spirit Guide
in the rhythm of tight-skinned drums
calling me to follow footpaths
sprinkled with ancient sea memories.
By faith I cling to unyielding rock,
fleshy fingers groping for secret places
high above the Devil's Ribbon.
Pricklypear tear at skin and soul,
create wounds not easily healed.
Sparrow hawks scream their need for prey,
snakes fall from the sky with no warning.
Following the trails of flint-footed goats,
I seek shelter under hovering stone
where black and red shadows leap from walls
in cactus-crowned visions of spirit dances.
I confront the beast that would steal my breath
to fill the cavern of the serpent's whiskered jaws.

continued

"Anasazi," plaster gauze, acrylic paints, Anasazi beans, malachite, jasper, dried grass and berries, horsetail, feathers, wooly mammoth ivory, sea shell, waxed linen thread.

White Shaman,
Your people's courage transfuses my soul,
echoes your pulse in the murmur of hummingbirds
weaving nests of tiny thorns and flaxen goat hair,
spinning cradles for seed-sized eggs,
pregnant promises for all Ages.
I feel their wisdom in lizards
languishing on warm pocked rocks,
luring me into the sun's embrace
where your Shadow Spirit rises
from a cylinder of stone.
The river reed sings your people's past,
haunting faded bluffs on desert breath.
The present is told by great blue herons
gathered beneath bridges and crumbling caves.
A papoose wrapped in the night's black blanket,
I see the future in a comet's white fire.

Man-in-the-Moon's Breath

On sleepless nights his music rises,
notes like stars begging
light from the night

daring me to close my eyes

spin in orbits of rhythm and blues,
ride long low-notes on cobalt haze,
taste bent string's ache for outer limits

constellations converge above our bed

echoing his return, heavy,
skin damp, fingers still seeking
full-again moons.

Summer Seductions

You looked like the old man Mom said you would —
eyes empty, color pale and dry like onion skin.
Vulnerable in the wake of surgeon's skill,
we closed windows on day's devouring heat,
refusing night's humid kiss on sterile sheets.
Suns rose and set behind ears of jackrabbits
we no longer saw from deserted porches.
Unheard hummingbirds murmured in flowers,
whippoorwills echoed, silent in our nights.

We could have heard the thunder-rumbles
lumbering over hills like lazy locomotives —
we could have smelled rain's kiss,
earth's submissive green moan.
But we shut all that was open,
cranked up the a/c,
conserving your energy,
consuming mine.

Lovers

Lover Sun feeds
fever's flash points,
ignites seeds in liquid fire.
Burning tongue
consumes want,
leaving ashes blown
on *Santa Ana* winds.

Lover Moon languishes
in hollows, desires
warmth like a moth
seeks flame.
Crescent flesh rises
on salty shores,
creates tides moaning
la luna.

One follows
neither leads,
twin footsteps
Apollo, Artemis.
Unable to love
one without
the other,
I do not choose.

"Lovers," plaster gauze, handmade hand-painted papers, foil paper, aluminum foil, acrylic paint.

Testimonials

I didn't say *You owe us this*
this chardonnay, this treehouse,
this moon on Cinnamon Bay.
I didn't watch you snorkel
Water Lemon Key,
an out-of-breath sea horse
too tired for the chase.
I didn't dream a single nightmare,
despite mosquito-net ghosts
above our bed.

I did say *Let's spend the money*
make mango-berry rum drinks,
wear hibiscus in our hair.
I did watch hermit crabs creep
past bay rum trees, shells on backs,
back to seas that birthed us all.
I did get lei'd at Duffy's Love Shack,
stuff myself with fat conch fritters,
make love in our patio hot tub
in front of God and everybody.

Hero's Goodnight

Moon sheds its shadow,
snake its skin —
neither, naked.

What of heroes who slip from myth
on journeys through the corridor?
Egos glorify adventures,
totality of triumphs —
echoes of bravado.

Once conquered
dragon does not rise,
black knight's sword is still,
maiden is no virgin,
mountain does not beckon.

With nothing left to rescue,
snake bids goodnight to moon.

Copper Canyon

Bound by velvet, mahogany, windows,
I hold my breath, waiting for sky,
ready to fly with green parrots over poinsettias
running the rails, deep into canyon-sliced mountains,
jungles camouflaged in their own opulence,
a plume of black smoke feathering our wake.

Our guide bursts in, the smile of youth
igniting her eyes, pleading my mouth
to mirror hers half my age, she grabs my hand, urging
kisses on dry pale cheeks of those abandoned,
we bump and nudge our way through each coach,
leaving conditioned air for a new world of chickens
and children, and brown-skinned faces
broad as plates, the smell of working
and living with little regret.

The guide babbles about bribes, unbelievable views,
tugging me farther from the things I know
or thought I knew, past old men sleeping,
their newspaper bibs rising, falling with each breath,
past a baby at her mother's breast, no bib at all
to stem the stream that runs between them,
drawing me, drawing me forward to a past
I've never known.

My escort greets the engineer with a flurry of Spanish
Buenos días, señor, esto es magnífico! Gracias,
muchas gracias and pushes me through the small door
opening onto yet another world rushing
to receive me, lifting my hair straight out behind me,
filling my lungs with a sharpness and just the hint
of something bitter.

46

Inching forward on a catwalk siding
I seek the platform at the engine's point,
a buffer between the journey and what might lie
on the track, vibrations throbbing through my hands,
hands groping the belly of the beast propelling
me into black-mouthed caves, across trestles
bridging leafy canopies, meandering rivers,
a new way of seeing the world, I reach
the destination duly bargained for,
camera hanging from my neck, a black albatross
incapable of soaring out to meet the moment,
to take it home to those who could not make the trip.

For once, I do not hide behind it, snapping pictures
of what I cannot see, or touch, or feel.
It is the ride of a lifetime, this lifetime's ride,
faster than ever before, but this time,
this time seeing, touching, feeling
everything.

Claiming Autumn

Rusty rainfalls lay
cypress needle
carpet runners
down the Guadalupe.
This river calls to me
just as she called
over a century ago
to shingle makers
seeking cypress hearts
along her mossy banks.

She invites me
to walk water,
river of forgotten sins,
mistakes, dreams.
I accept the invitation,
walk water, claim autumn,
its red oak hot flashes
igniting cedar hills,
its pyracantha clots
dripping from fence posts,
its lost maple flames
licking cottonwood clouds.

I walk with the current
away from the past,
embracing north winds
to strip me bare,
naked again,
the way I entered
this world,
crying,
no regrets.

San Solomon's Spell

Listen for whispers carried
on wind, tales of conquistadors,
French traders, settlers, the telling told
on nights like these, campfires' burnt
offerings reflecting the stars.

Migrate with Monarchs seeking
longer days and warmer nights.
Lie wrapped in the past
under cottonwood canopies braced
by bark thick with desire.

Make love for three days,
quarter moon rising
on mountains draped in indigo secrets,
breezes seduced by coyotes' call,
history dissolved in a desert.

The Weight of Ashes

for Sally

I wake with ringing in my ears,
the scent of desert on my skin,
a thirst so strong I cannot hope.
Through the open window

I inhale your gifts,
sage, santolina, salvia,
their aromas rising with the sun,
too soon devoured by the heat.

I resist getting out of bed,
afraid to rouse the sleeping grief,
the weight of your ashes too heavy.
The children, our friends, they call,

I don't respond, I am sleeping.
I dream the earth is my blanket,
you kiss me goodnight.

Breath Found Along the Way

In the beginning, itself an ending,
I wore grief like a mask
cast with my own hands,
layer on layer, memories'
fingers crafting the distance
between myself and me.
Immeasurable, I yearned to evaporate
like morning fog on the Guadalupe.

Sinking instead, I gasped for breath,
desperate to take one last gulp.
Drowning, I learned to receive, not take,
the breath that was mine —
that the Universe exhaled, just for me,
waiting, waiting, for me to receive,
to inhale the gift, always mine.

I learned to erase the lines,
to feel the flow of one into other,
a river's journey through the past
now moving into what will be.
All green, all liquid, all One.
I learned to listen for breath,
the flow within myself, the *chi*.

I know my own breath now,
its flow from who I was,
who I am, who I am yet to be.
I let my mask fall, it sinks
like a stone,
is gone.

Reading Music

Two decades between us,
how will I know you
in the years to come
when body language
ceases cues I've come
to know so well,
to count on?

I will read you still,
even while your fingers
cannot find the strings —
remembering your music,
its pull at my heart,
always telling me
what I need to know.

Anniversary

for Harry

I still yearn for you, like a priest yearns
for sinners to herald his own salvation,
praying for forgiveness in a darkened closet.

I still ache for you, like a gypsy aches
for backroads tracking full-moon promises
over the next horizon.

I still hunger for you, like harmonicas hunger
for blues to wail into the night,
moaning with a long low cry when sun insists on rising.

I still thirst for you, like the desert thirsts
for rain to swell its cactus soul,
urging bursts of startled bloom above its thorny bed.

I still celebrate you, like a child celebrates
Christmas under the evergreen tree,
believing in faith that next year
reindeer will return.

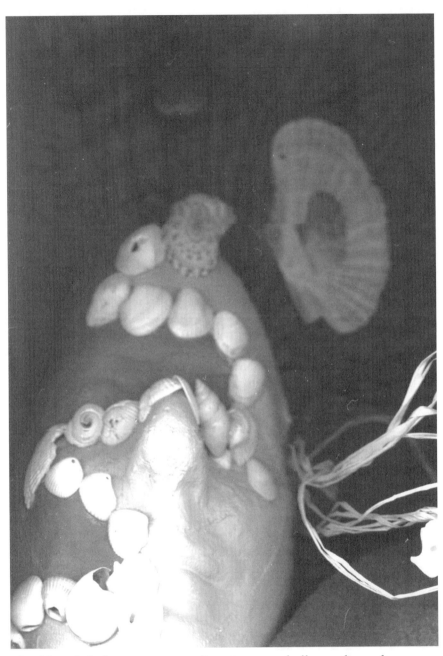

"Sea Nymph," plaster gauze, acrylic paints, sea shells, sea fan, rafia.

Swimming Lessons

I should've guessed he'd live on an island,
sleep next to a kinky-haired woman who
tall and hipless like their cottage palms,
knows how to bend in the wind.
No gold band to interrupt fingers,
they peel flesh from papayas
and circumnavigate coral beds
blooming in the sun.

I should've seen it coming,
that weak moment he flew south
to reconcile his mother's dreams of
Caribbean cruises, a son who loves her.
He sailed by chance, banked on sand dollars,
sent mom back home alone.

I should've snagged him when we first met,
before he bolted for Alaska,
the last frontier,
where hearts and suns sleep all winter,
where land is cheap and people scarce
as lovers' words from a Jeep's back seat.

I should've said then
You'll go too far,
a place too cold
for things you claim to need.
What did I know? I learned to juggle
kids, carpools, Hamburger Helper.

Two oceans ago we dated once,
when I should've learned to swim.

San Antonio Birthday

You delight me
with dancing bananas,
surprise me
with whispered wishes,

a walk along the river
weaving magic
in and out the crowd,
my hand secure in yours.

Road Games

I spy something
falling from the sky,
clutch of feathers refusing
release before the rising
earth swallows them both,

but it doesn't,

the hawks uncouple,
fly separate skies.
I turn up the radio's CW songs,
a reminder I'm not alone.

I spy something
shivering on cottonwoods,
bleached by the sun,
held fast by bark thick with age.
Sky behind the leaves looks empty

but it's not,

I paint it with color and clouds,
rusty reds that keep me grounded,
real enough to sign my name.

I spy something
growing in snow pockets,
thorny skin numbed, green,
still promising blooms.
Mesquite tree beyond them looks dead

but it's not,

its taproot snaking where waters run deep.
I check my map, circle
landmarks I need
to remember.

Extravagance

A friend calls me extravagant,
maybe I am.
At 48, I refuse anymore
to buy cheap toilet paper.
Discounting differences, we stroll shops,
I fondle baubles and beads
warm with amber like tigers' eyes.
Sun in the palms of my hands,
I step out on the sidewalk to bask.
Aren't they great? I prompt.
Lovely she whispers.

We stop to stroke fabrics,
racks of them hanging-out
for attention, like children,
some subtle, some shouting,
all anxious to be noticed.
My friend's hand lingers
on a shimmer of swirls,
turquoise and purple,
an elegant bruise in need of caress.

A man once gave me a shawl
my friend lifts the hanger,
fingertips tracing promises
across a peacock's tail.
Like this? I prod,
hoping she won't drift away.
A long time ago
she releases the cloth
sifting like sand through her fingers
one summer in Morocco.

My friend rehangs the dress,
arranges its proper lines.
I'd love to see it, I press,
knowing she's already gone.
I don't still have it, Silly,
retreat complete behind crooked smile
what would I do with it now?

Billboard

SPANK YOUR SENSES
WITH PEPSI KONA COFFEE COLA
bold letters scream above the streets,
vying for my attention — the light is red,
the audience captive.

Streaking on cue,
he appears in the intersection,
worn leather and rusted metal
groan in tandem as he pops a wheelie,
extending his hand palm-up
in an awkward finale.

He rolls my way,
I avoid the eyes above his
cardboard-scribbled *Vietnam Vet* —
too close to seeing my own reflection,
I turn to search the sidewalk,
waiting for the green light
to signal my escape.
The light changes,
I never look back.

Back Country

Rusted tin roofs
run in corrugated rows
like wrinkled foreheads
above sagging cabin faces.

Phoenix 2001

Chanting his due date like a mantra
against summer's heat,
we waited nearly nine months.
He arrived two weeks early.
His mother, heavy and ripe with waiting,
ready, too, when he entered our world wailing,
strong with new life's promise,
blessed by the love of family and friends
around the birthing bed.

We celebrated his coming
with the late August rain's cleansing
end to summer dog days.
A red-tailed hawk welcomed him home,
perching on a limb outside the house
like the momentary sun's messenger,
foreshadowing promises later sought
for the world's rise from the rubble
and reign of unholy ashes.

Marveling under perfection's spell
spun in tiny curled fingers,
no weight of the world
on feathered lashes closed in sleep,
his body still curved in womb's memory,
we snuggle him,
grateful for the two extra weeks
to this very day
marked on our calendars months ago,
September 11,
a doctor's guess at advent.

An early morning phone call
dispels the home-bound magic.
We turn on TV with an urgency
not felt in weeks,

watching the screen,
horror growing in our bellies,
disbelief rising in our throats,
cries strangled above the infant's head
My God, what's happening?
How can this be happening?

My daughter weeps.
Her husband takes their son from her arms,
carrying the weight of fellow firemen,
he walks away without words for the tears
running down his face and into his sleeping son's,
unable to answer his wife's question
Why in the name of God did we bring a child
into this world?

The wisdom I share with this new mother
is not mine, it echoes in my heart
from all the grandmothers that go before me,
ones who have loved and lost their own,
knowing that love is never lost,
that the world continues in the breath of children,
yours, mine, ours –
they rise
our only hope.

In Time For Dinner

I saw him again yesterday,
shuffling behind bumpers
in Wal-Mart's parking lot.
His feet refusing to defy
gravity or the growing stain
around his zipper,
its warm race down his legs.
Couldn't read that face,
dry and cracked
like an old creekbed.
He never hesitated,
just followed the trail
in his head.

He did find his truck,
testimonial no doubt,
to the years they'd shared.
He fumbled for the bull's-eye
winking at his keys.
I almost went to help him,
but he managed on his own,
pitched plastic bags
across the cab,
hauled himself in, groaned.

I watched him sag
to catch his breath
before poking at the dash.
The pick-up coughed,
then shuddered,
sounding terminal to me.
I couldn't help
but wait.

He stared out the windshield,
a dusty cobweb of glittery cracks;
diagnosing or daydreaming,
I couldn't tell which.
He tried again,
no better luck,
and leaned to rest
against the wheel.

I came closer,
afraid he'd never
raise his head.
Can I help you, sir?
My voice a hollow echo,
even in my ears.

Like a hound disturbed
from his afternoon nap,
he barely raised his head.
Offering me a smile, he said
Nope, but thank you kindly, ma'am.
This ol' truck still gits me there . . .
He tickled keys, reluctant parts responding.
. . . see there, and back in time for dinner.

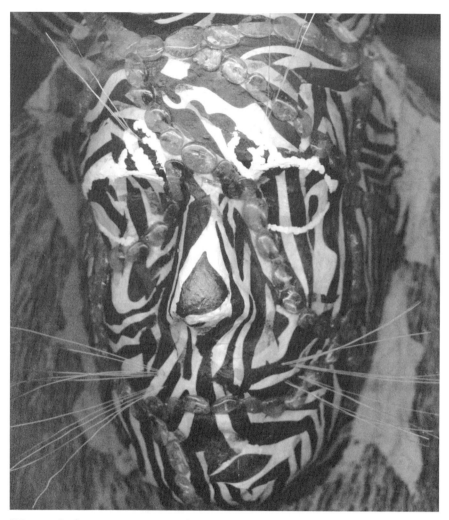

"Tigress," plaster gauze, printed tissue paper, amber beads, broomstraw wreath, acrylic paint, synthetic whiskers. Thanks to Linda Karst Stone for technical design assistance.

Excorcism

I wake in a trembling bed,
moon-ribbons sliced across our sheets.
You quiver beneath your skin
like a cat curled in on itself.

I wait for your tremors to calm,
to leave you in peace,
to welcome my sleep's return
lost in your white cotton wake.

Reaching to stroke your arm,
I listen for rhythm's breath.
Full moon yields to clouded shroud,
we sink in a dark sea of sheets.

Soft snores drift in the midnight air,
leaving me in wonder.
Demons dispelled by just a touch?
I fall asleep, purring, beside you.

Christmas Carol

It's Christmas in the kitchen
and Grandma's drinkin' wine,
Mogen David Blackberry,
inspirin' pies divine.

Buddy's brought a tree in,
Sis is stringin' lights,
grandkids hoop and holler,
dancin' their delight.

Grandma sits and smiles now,
smoke-wreath 'round her head,
tokin' on her Winston,
sippin' jelly jars of red.

It's Christmas in the kitchen,
nothin's fancy but it's fine —
the table's set and ready,
it's Grandma's turn to shine.

Guitar Man

Using darkness as a balm
I stroke your body,
light touch yearning
for places I can't reach.
There's no familiar answer
rising hard beneath my fingers,
only an instinctive quiver
dissolving in the night.

Like the wind before a storm,
your mood changes,
a sudden shift, variable and gusty.
Recognizing the threat of thunder,
I reach for the light, still
believing in its power over dark.

Shunning shadows, you slip away,
answering whispers on a moonlit porch,
beckonings only you can hear.
You caress the slender neck, coax
melodies from hand-carved curves.
I listen from our room
for the song you cannot sing.

Too Much Information

If this were a movie
and if we smoked,
this is the scene
where we'd roll over,
light a cigarette,
inquire
Was it as good for you
as it was for me?
and the smoke rings would hover
like drunken angels circling, colliding,
disbanding in the dark.

But this isn't a movie,
we aren't smokers,
and I'm not ready
for this scene to be over.
Drawing in my arms and knees,
frog-like I press against
your sides, warm and wet
I sink against your chest.

Inhaling you,
the smell of me on you,
I feel the shift
beneath my body's weight,
your breathing long and deep,
my head rising in cadence
with your lungs.
I tease your nipple
with my fingertip,
soft, light, barely there.

Man, *oh man, if your Mother*
only knew
you stroke my hair,
I burrow deeper, smiling
at the thought of Mom here,
in our bedroom,
behind the potted plant
or in the corner
on the overstuffed chair.
I whisper *That's T-M-I for Mom*
and wriggle backwards
to slick your body with my tongue,
lingering on your navel
before I roll over
to crab for the sheets
with my toes.

What the hell is T-M-I?

How could he not
remember Too Much Information?
T-M-I the kids' standard chant
when Aunt Fran
shared on morning constitutionals
and why exactly
they were so important,
their *T-M-I* chorus during
Grandma's discussions
of so and so's childbirth
with all the particulars,
their moan of *T-M-I*
if we even hinted at a nap
in the middle of the afternoon.

continued

You roll over like a slow-motion
wave, sliding one arm beneath
my back, the other across my breasts.
Too much information
you remember, your breath
lingers in my ear, your hand
resting on my breast
with the weight of an infant
almost asleep.

Kids think they're grown up
before they grow up
I don't answer your pillow mumbles,
don't let you know on this one
I may have to side with the kids —

like when the newscaster reads
with a face as blank as his voice,
cataloguing the condition
of the seventh victim
of the latest serial killer,

or when my ex-roommate stops me
in the grocery store
on the feminine hygiene aisle
to inform on her lying, cheating,
S. O. B. husband,

or if someone wants to talk
about games
grown daughters play
beneath the sheets,
that's all just T-M-I.

"Memories," aluminum foil (from plaster gauze cast), cardboard, spray
paints, jewelry, shell, found objects.

Wellsprings

Wise women weep well,
howling at an empty sky —
no anguish, just challenge
You will not swallow me today!

Wise women feel pain,
bearing it in their bones
and in their wombs,
a frame of reference,
their source of power.

Hunger's Need

Your nest is fragile,
no longer warmed by the familiar.
Hunger wells up within you
like a scream, a great, yawning
emptiness waiting to be filled —
a need to know patterns
filigreed on leaves,
to fly above the river's fingers
on the breath of summer.

Dressed in feathers, soft
like dandelion fuzz in peril
of being lost to the wind's restless tug,
you wait to be filled —
always open, wanting more,
needing to feed the ember
growing larger every day.

Nothing Like

I learned to cut vegetables carelessly,
nothing like the ones from my mother's kitchen
carefully measured
in even lengths
all the same thickness.

I protested at first, *They won't cook evenly.*
And so? he'd say, and chop away.
But some will be done
and some will be raw.

And that's a problem?
I thought so.

I learned it's so easy
to hack with abandon,
passion-speak Rilke to Rumi
Aristotle to Plato,
glasses of wine
flanking the cutting boards,
Bose blaring Three Tenors,
Vivaldi, Sor.

Nothing like my mother's kitchen.

Porch Sitting

I used to seek sunsets,
their great, glorious bursts of color,
preferring now the silence of salvia,
letting their scarlet crowns seduce me
as well as the hummingbirds.

Cedar blankets cover hills to the east,
wrapping me in their muted comfort-colors,
allowing the day to slip into twilight's
dull memory of sun, its caress light,
soft, still warm — reaching me
where I need to be touched.

Jail House Rock

Judge, jury, jailer — all inmates
in my head, the years making them
more reserved, less resolute, not so rowdy.
But they're still there, ready to condemn
my pen on paper, fingers at keyboard,
their tongues loose, their lips moving.

Whispers sound like mother's hiss
What will the neighbors think?
Others just sigh and summon daddy,
his head in his hands, hiding eyes
but not disappointment. Brother grumbles
You make granny sound like a lush
while sister accuses *That's a lie —*
you never write the truth!

Ex-husband testifies *I brought home my paycheck,*
what else did you want? prompting current mate
to raise his brow, but not his voice, continuing
to read the record. Daughters gasp *T-M-I!*
Just too much information, Mom!
Old friend whines *THAT was a secret*
while Father Flynn cross-examines
Why weren't you attending Mass
instead of shaman caves?

Some days I'm a stronger witness,
telling them all to shut up, slamming the door
shut on them all. But sometimes, sometimes
I'm just too tired, or they're too loud,
or one of them has their foot in the door
and I can't quite get it closed to lock them in –
or out.

continued

And even if I can, they press against the bars,
all yelling and shouting *Irrelevant! Hearsay! I object!*
stretching out long arms between bars, hands grabbing,
fingers pinching, pulling, pissing me off until I scream
Enough! Enough! To hell with you all!
throwing down pen, punching off computer,
making my escape to the front porch to rock —
praying for the death sentence.

Tortuga Del Mar

She traded her wedding band for the blue amber ring,
imagining on its surface a woman striding into the sea,
a delicious freedom set in stone.

Her dreams filled with sea turtles, their great green backs
beneath her feet, seaweed reins in her trembling hands,
the ride on parting waves taking her out to sea.

Daughters on the beach cried *Mommy! Mommy!*
unheard for the ocean's song filling her ears with screeching
gulls and surf-pounding rhythms long forgotten.

Arms and legs ached with the horizon's approach,
sun's need burning alabaster skin until she cried out *Mama!*
just once, before plunging through blue amber waves

to the new place she would call home.

Birdsong

thanks to Frank

Joseph Byrd was discovered in his workshop,
body slumped slightly,
head neatly resting
between the awls and knives
arranged according to size.
In his open hand,
a piece of maplewood,
the promises of butterscotch slivers
collecting like curled down
around his feet.

Joseph Byrd would have chosen the wood carefully,
analyzing curves and planes
the grain would accept
to create the creature anew,
sure in the wisdom
of his knife's flight
to find it there, hiding,
in its own nest.

Joseph Byrd carved away excess,
sanding wings so thin
the light behind them
passed like breath
between the feathers.
Polishing the amber breast
he brought fire to the wood's heart,
then quietly set it free.

Reasons for Leaving

1) We arrived here like refugees, desperate
for a new home, exhausted. We are no longer refugees.

2) The weight of this house and all its contents
is baggage we no longer need to claim.

3) This distance crafted between us is a road
we no longer care to travel day after day for those little necessities.

4) Rock and cedar once so inviting, no longer nurture.
The spring shrinks.

5) We have fasted and prayed in the desert,
no longer with need for penance.

Alphabet Soup

I eat bowls of alphabet soup,
watch letters stream
like bubbles from my fingertips,
word-drifts float across the page.

I wait for words
to dribble from my lips, salty runs
splash and pool between my breasts.

I taste names
fetticcini enchilada creole
roll them on my tongue like a chocolate kiss.

I smell spices
rise from unwritten poems,
rhythms simmering on a white paper stove.

I eat bowls of alphabet soup,
I am never full.

About the Poet

Photo by Rachel Krenek

Anne Schneider is a native Houstonian who grew up near the Shamrock Hilton and the Astrodome. After graduating from St. Agnes Academy in 1971, she attended the University of Texas. She raised two daughters, facilitated Scripture study classes, led Marriage Encounter and Engaged Sponsor programs for Holy Family Catholic Church in Missouri City, Texas, and was a Camp Fire leader and director of summer camps. From 1986 to 1995, she was Corporate Treasurer of Living Windows Corporation, her family's manufacturing business since 1958. After the sale of the company, she and her husband Harry built a log home near Hunt, Texas, above the North Fork of the Guadalupe River. They moved to the Texas Hill Country in 1995, where she has pursued full-time writing. Another move is imminent as they prepare to remodel an old home in the historic Methodist Encampment area at Mount Wesley in Kerrville, Texas.

As President of the Kerrville Writers Association since 1996, she has presented short story and poetry lectures in the community and was the director of Kerr County's Annual Students Short Story Contest for six years. In 1990, she was a finalist for Best Texas Short Stories. She has been editor and contributor for numerous Texas newsletters and her poetry has been published in journals and regional presses. **Breath Found Along the Way** is her first volume of poetry.

She translates her literary creativity into the visual arts through mask making. Since 1999, her face-casting mask workshops have been scheduled throughout south Texas and her masks have been exhibited in contemporary art galleries. Expanding her creative arts experience, she conducted her first SoulCatcher doll-making workshop in 2002 at the Hill Country Arts Foundation. Progressively playful, she is a charter member of the Hunt Chapter of Sweet Potato Queens International and appears in costume for parades and parties.

continued

She has been a student of *Tai Chi* since 1998, and daily practices *yoga* and *QiGong*. She is a volunteer leader for *Tai Chi* at Kerrville's Dietert Senior Center, and began teaching *Tai Chi* classes in a local art studio in 2001. She now teaches *Tai Chi* at Spirit Wind Java, a coffee shop and art space in Ingram, Texas.

For information on mask or doll workshops call 830-895-3361 during daylight hours or email: poetsmask@omniglobal.net.